Contents

Energy from inside atoms

Nuclear power comes from the energy inside atoms. The word 'nuclear' refers to the nucleus, or central core, of an atom. When atomic nuclei are forced to break apart, a tremendous amount of energy is released. The same is true if atomic nuclei are forced to join together.

Both these processes are nuclear reactions. The splitting reaction is called fission, and the joining is fusion. Nuclear power plants around the world today use controlled nuclear fission to produce energy that is turned into electricity.

Elements and atoms

All the world's matter – solids, liquids and gases – is made up of chemical elements. There are more than a hundred elements – such as iron, oxygen and silicon – and they cannot be broken down into simpler substances. Each is made up of atoms, which are the basic units of all matter. They are sometimes called the building blocks of the universe, because everything is made up of atoms. They are incredibly small. Their width ranges from about a tenth to half a nanometre (or billionth of a metre!).

Yet these tiny atoms are not simple particles. Each atom contains even smaller, subatomic particles. Some of these, called protons and neutrons, cluster together to form the atom's nucleus. Lighter particles, called electrons, circle around the nucleus (see diagram opposite). The atoms of each of the world's elements contain a different number of protons. For example, hydrogen – the lightest element – has just one proton, while oxygen has eight, silicon 14 and iron 26 protons. Hydrogen is an exceptional element, because it has no neutrons. All other elements have a number of neutrons as well as protons.

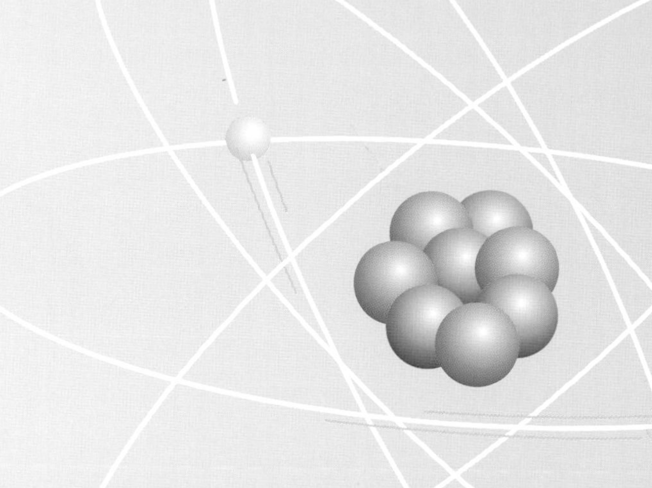

Subatomic particles called protons (red, in the cluster) carry a positive charge of electricity, and circling electrons carry a negative charge. Neutrons, as the name suggests, are neutral and carry no electric charge.

Different forms

Most elements can have more than one form, depending on the number of neutrons they have. The different forms are called isotopes. The most important element for the production of nuclear power – uranium (see page 14) – has 92 protons. Its most common isotope has 146 neutrons and is called uranium 238 (U-238 for short) because it has a total of 238 subatomic particles in its nucleus. But the uranium isotope most used in nuclear power stations has 143 neutrons and is called U-235.

Is nuclear power a natural force?

It is not only natural, it also creates all the energy we receive on Earth! That's because all the world's energy comes originally from nuclear reactions that take place in the central core of the Sun, our nearest star. The core is so hot and dense that the nuclei of hydrogen atoms join together to form nuclei of another, heavier gas – helium – which has two protons. This nuclear fusion produces enormous amounts of energy, which the Sun gives off as light and heat. On Earth, radioactive decay (see page 8) also happens naturally.

Radioactive decay

As well as fission and fusion, a third nuclear reaction gives off energy. Most isotopes are stable, which means that their nuclei do not break apart unless energy is supplied by outside forces. But some isotopes are unstable. These isotopes have nuclei that break down on their own to form smaller groups of particles. These unstable forms are called radioactive isotopes, because when they break apart they give off energy in the form of radiation. Uranium, radium and radon are elements with unstable isotopes. They give off energy and contribute to the natural background radiation that is always present on Earth.

This new symbol warns people of deadly radiation and tells them to move away quickly.

Small doses of natural radiation are not harmful to people, even over a long period. But exposure to the high levels of radiation given off by nuclear fission and fusion can damage body cells, leading to serious illness and even death. That is one reason to be very careful with nuclear energy.

Controlled and uncontrolled reactions

When a nucleus splits in a fission reaction, it gives off neutrons. These neutrons then bombard and split other nuclei, setting up a series of fissions. The process can be repeated over and over again, creating a chain reaction and giving off an enormous amount of energy. In nuclear power stations, the chain reaction is carefully controlled so that energy is released slowly.

An uncontrolled chain reaction can lead to a devastating explosion. This is how the fission devices of nuclear weapons work. The chain reaction can take place in less than one millionth of a second, creating enormous amounts of energy all at once. The explosion also gives off radiation that strikes dust and other particles in the air, and these fall back to the ground as nuclear

Dealing with the dangers

People tend to be either very strongly in favour of, or completely against using nuclear power stations to generate electricity. Both sides have convincing arguments. There is a link between nuclear-produced electricity and nuclear weapons, simply because the science behind them is the same. Pro-nuclear groups believe the dangers of this link are exaggerated, while their opponents deny this. The British environmental scientist James Lovelock writes: 'We must conquer our fears and accept nuclear energy as the one safe and proven energy source that has minimal global consequences. It is now as reliable as any human engineering can be and has the best safety record of all large-scale energy sources.' On the other hand, international environmental organization Greenpeace says, 'Greenpeace has always fought – and will continue to fight – vigorously against nuclear power because it is an unacceptable risk to the environment and to humanity.'

fallout. This fallout is very damaging to humans. The atomic bombs which were dropped on the Japanese cities of Hiroshima and Nagasaki in 1945 were fission devices. Fusion reactions can also be controlled, but have not yet been used successfully for power production (see page 41). Uncontrolled nuclear fusion is used in weapons. Weapons called thermonuclear devices combine nuclei under intense heat. They are even more destructive than fission devices.

A nuclear explosion at the US test site in Nevada in 1951. It was caused by dropping a bomb code-named Charlie from a B-50 aircraft.

The growth of atomic science

Modern atomic science began in the early nineteenth century, when the English chemist John Dalton (1766-1844) stated that chemical elements were made of tiny particles called atoms. But the idea of atoms had been proposed more than 2000 years earlier, by the ancient Greek philosopher Democritus (460-370 BC). It was he who named the tiny particles atoms, from the Greek for 'indivisible'.

Democritus believed that everything in the world was made up of a different combination of these particles. Dalton realized that each chemical element is composed of its own kind of atoms. But he continued with the same mistaken belief – that atoms cannot be divided.

Discovering radioactivity

The study of nuclear energy began with the discovery of radioactivity in 1896 by the French physicist Henri Becquerel (1852-1908). He found that uranium ore gave off energy in the form of invisible rays, when he saw that uranium affected a photographic plate. His work was carried on by the Polish-born French scientist Marie Curie (1867-1934), who discovered two new radioactive elements, radium (from the word ray) and polonium (named after Marie's homeland of Poland).

Nuclear physics

The science of nuclear physics began in 1911, when the New Zealand-born British physicist Ernest Rutherford (1871-1937) discovered that all atoms have a heavy central core, later called the nucleus. He also found that the core was surrounded by a cloud of orbiting particles – electrons. Rutherford won a Nobel Prize for chemistry for his work and became known as the father of nuclear science.

Other scientists worked on the question of nuclear energy. The German-born physicist Albert Einstein (1879-1955) worked out that the mass (or amount

Why make an atomic bomb?

Early nuclear physicists did not set out to create weapons. Many of them were most interested in pure research, gaining knowledge for its own sake. In America, many scientists were refugees from Nazi Germany, and they knew that other German scientists might be working towards developing an atomic bomb. In 1939, Einstein wrote to President Roosevelt, warning of this. The Second World War broke out in September that year, and this meant that nuclear science was directed towards bombs. The race was on to be the first to develop atomic weapons. Perhaps this would have happened anyway, whenever nuclear fission was achieved, but it was accelerated by the Second World War. For this reason, nuclear technology will always be linked to weapons of mass destruction in many people's minds.

of matter) in atoms can change into energy. He also created a formula for calculating the amount of atomic energy released. This was the equation $E = mc^2$. It showed that energy (E) equals mass (m) multiplied by the speed of light (c) multiplied by itself (^{2}). Einstein's work showed that the energy released by atomic changes, such as splitting a nucleus, is enormous. Scientists later discovered that splitting one kilogram of uranium releases the same energy as igniting 16 million kilograms of high explosive (TNT). This led on to the first atomic bomb.

Albert Einstein explains another equation during a lecture at the California Institute of Technology in 1931.

The start of the nuclear age

During the 1930s, scientists discovered a great deal about atomic structure. They tried to split the nuclei of atoms by bombarding them with neutron particles. In 1938 a group of German and Austrian physicists and chemists, led by Otto Hahn (1879-1968), split the nucleus of an atom in uranium. Other scientists wondered if the neutrons that broke away from a nucleus could be used to split another nucleus and set up a chain reaction. Italian-born physicist Enrico Fermi (1901-54) led a team at the University of Chicago which tried to create a nuclear chain reaction. They built their device, called an atomic pile, beneath the stands of the sports field. The pile contained 45 tonnes of uranium and uranium oxide. In December 1942, it produced the first successful controlled chain reaction.

The first atomic bombs

In 1942 the United States government set up a top-secret programme to develop an atomic bomb. Called the Manhattan Project, it was led by physicist J. Robert Oppenheimer (1904-67) at Los Alamos in the

An engineer checks a reconstruction of one of Enrico Fermi's original atomic piles in 1956.

This photograph was taken inside the Calder Hall nuclear power station a year after it went into operation.

New Mexico desert. Many top American scientists were involved and, on 16 July 1945, the world's first atom bomb was exploded at Trinity Site in New Mexico. Nuclear energy was as powerful in reality as it seemed in theory. The following month, US planes dropped atomic bombs on the Japanese cities of Hiroshima and Nagasaki, killing at least 140,000 people. The Japanese surrendered soon afterwards, and President Truman said, "I realize the tragic significance of the atomic bomb."

A non-renewable resource

Resources are called renewable if they are inexhaustible and we don't reduce stocks when we use them. Solar, wind, water, geothermal and biomass power are all renewable. But nuclear power is not, because nuclear fuel is used up to produce energy. The uranium used as fuel is mined from underground, and once all the uranium has been used, there won't be any more. This is also the case with other non-renewable resources, such as coal, oil and natural gas. Other radioactive elements may be used in future, but they will still be non-renewable.

Nuclear power plants

After the Second World War, scientists worked on using nuclear energy to produce electricity. An experimental reactor was used to generate electricity in Idaho, USA, in 1951. Two years later, US President Eisenhower was so impressed that he made a speech called 'Atoms for Peace', urging the use of nuclear power. It quickly became an international issue, and in 1954 the Soviet Union opened its first experimental nuclear power plant. Then, in 1956, came the world's first full-scale commercial nuclear plant, Calder Hall in Sellafield, England. Eventually, four reactors were built on the site, which operated until 2003.

How the nuclear fuel cycle works

The nuclear fuel cycle is a series of linked processes that produce electricity in nuclear reactors. The cycle begins with the mining of uranium ore. This is processed and then used as nuclear fuel. After the uranium has been used to produce electricity, some of the spent fuel is reprocessed so that it can go back to a reactor, beginning the cycle all over again. Fuel which cannot be reprocessed is waste and has to be disposed of.

Mining uranium

Uranium is a heavy, silvery-white metal found in the Earth's crust. It is about as common as tin and 500 times more common than gold. The uranium is in ores that are obtained from different kinds of rocks. It was first found in 1789 in pitchblende, which is still the most important source of uranium ore, along with carnotite, sandstone and uraninite.

Nearly half the world's uranium ore comes from underground mines. Miners or remote-controlled drills remove the ore in chunks, which are brought to the surface. About a quarter comes from open-pit mines, where large holes are dug in the surface. Another quarter comes from solution mining, in which a liquid is pumped through the ore to dissolve it.

More than half the world's uranium deposits are mined in three countries – Canada, Australia and Kazakhstan. The largest mine is in Canada: the McArthur River underground mine produces more than 18 per cent of the world total. The box (right) shows the top ten producers in 2006.

WORLD URANIUM PRODUCERS

Country	%
Canada	25.0
Australia	19.3
Kazakhstan	13.4
Niger	8.7
Russia	8.3
Namibia	7.8
Uzbekistan	5.7
USA	4.2
Ukraine	2.0
China	1.9
Total	**96.3**

The diagram shows the complete nuclear fuel cycle. This includes supplying nuclear fuel to the power plant and disposing of used fuel. The cycle begins with mining ore and ends with burying nuclear waste.

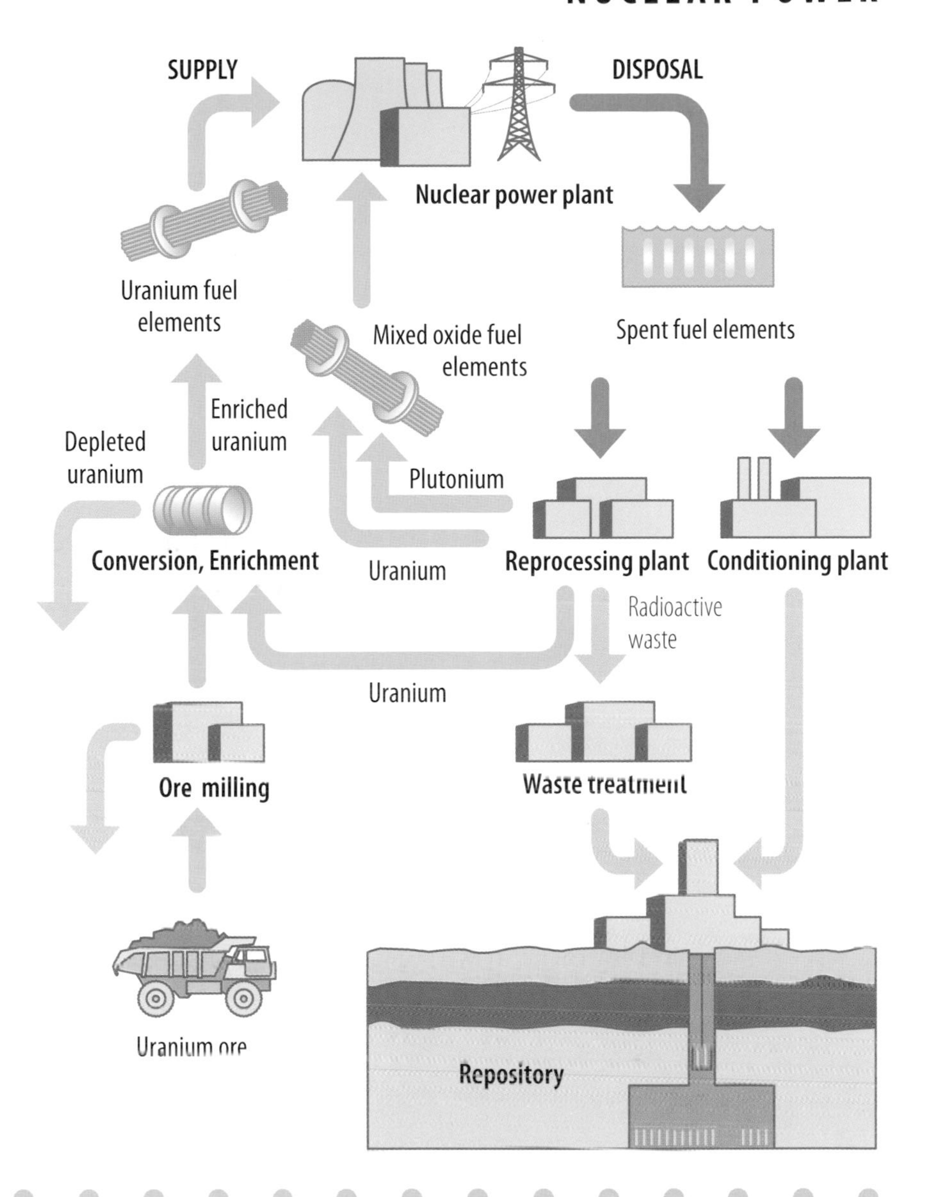

Making yellowcake

The chunks of ore are milled at a plant near the mine. Here the ore is crushed, ground and treated with chemicals to produce a concentrated uranium oxide called yellowcake. The uranium in yellowcake is generally made up of 0.7 per cent U-235 and 99.3 per cent U-238. Fission reactors need a higher percentage of U-235, so the uranium next has to be converted and enriched.

Is uranium mining dangerous?

It is as dangerous as any ore mining, with the added hazard that uranium ore gives off radon gas. This is radioactive and can cause cancer. During the 1950s a number of American uranium miners developed lung cancer, and the nuclear industry says that it has taken steps to make sure that this no longer occurs. Today there are more safety checks, better ventilation in mines and miners handle the uranium less. The World Nuclear Association says: 'In the last 40 years, individual mining operations have been larger, and efficient ventilation and other precautions now protect underground miners from these hazards. Open cut mining of uranium virtually eliminates the danger. There has been no known case of illness caused by radiation among uranium miners in Australia or Canada. While this may be partly due to the lack of detailed information on occupational health from operations in the 1950s, it is clear that no major occupational health effects have been experienced in either country.'

Enriching the yellowcake

At a conversion plant, yellowcake is treated with various chemicals, including nitric acid. This produces uranium hexafluoride gas (UF_6, called hex), which is sent in metal containers to an enrichment plant. There the hex is processed to increase the concentration of U-235 from 0.7 to between 2 and 5 per cent. This process removes a large proportion of the U-238 using centrifuge or diffusion techniques.

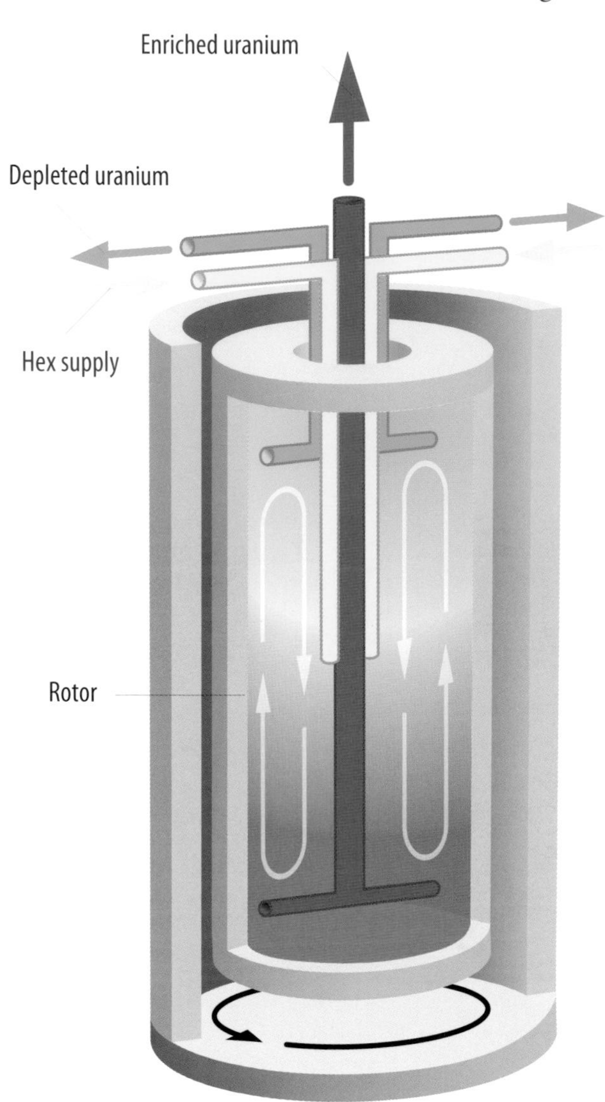

The diagram shows how the spinning rotor of a gas centrifuge produces enriched uranium. The depleted gas collects near the top of the centrifuge and the enriched uranium near the bottom, where it moves up through the red pipe.

A centrifuge spins the hex gas at very high speeds, separating the lighter U-235 from the denser U-238. The process is repeated several times, producing both enriched and depleted uranium (the latter is used in munitions such as shells). The diffusion method uses pumps to force the gas through millions of tiny holes, which the lighter U-235 passes through more easily. This uses much more energy than the centrifuge and will be used less in future.

There are other ways to enrich uranium, including using lasers to separate the different isotopes. France, Germany, the Netherlands, Russia, the UK and the USA all have large commercial enrichment plants, and there are smaller plants elsewhere.

Producing fuel

The enriched hex gas is converted to uranium dioxide (UO_2) powder at a fuel fabrication plant. The powder is pressed into cylindrical pellets and then baked at a very high temperature (1400°C). The pellets are sealed in metal tubes to form fuel rods up to five metres long, which are grouped in assemblies (or bundles) of 30 to 300, ready for use in a nuclear reactor. According to the World Nuclear

Fuel rods are stored in a cooling pool at a nuclear power plant in Virginia, USA.

Association, the process results in enriched nuclear fuel which represents about 0.135 per cent of the original mined uranium ore.

What happens to the ore

Mining
1000 tonnes of mined uranium ore...

Milling
...produces 11.5 tonnes of uranium oxide concentrate (yellowcake)...

Conversion
...creates 14.4 tonnes of uranium hexafluoride gas...

Enrichment
...produces 1.75 tonnes of enriched uranium hexafluoride...

Fuel fabrication
...makes 1.35 tonnes of uranium dioxide

Fuel for power or weapons?

Enriched uranium is used for both power generation and weapons. But nuclear reactors use low enriched uranium fuel (3-5 per cent U-235), while nuclear weapons need highly-enriched uranium (85 per cent or more U-235). The processes are the same, which is why people are concerned about enrichment. Will the enriched uranium be used to produce energy or weapons? This question is behind the anxiety around the world after Iran announced the opening of a nuclear reactor.

The Iranians say their intentions are peaceful and their nuclear reactor will soon produce electricity. The reactor was begun with German help in 1974 and resumed with Russian help in 1992. In December 2007 the Russians began delivering enriched uranium to Iran. The 1970 Treaty on the Non-Proliferation of Nuclear Weapons (see page 35), states that all countries have the right to use nuclear technology peacefully, but not to build nuclear weapons.

What happens inside a nuclear reactor

Bundles of fuel rods are placed in the core of a nuclear reactor. The core needs a specific quantity of fuel to set up and maintain a chain reaction. This quantity of fuel is called the critical mass. The U-235 nuclei then split, giving off enormous energy as heat, which boils water to produce steam. Some of the U-238 in the fuel turns into plutonium, which also splits and produces energy.

To control the chain reaction, the core also has long metal control rods containing materials such as boron or cadmium. These substances absorb neutrons and they can be pushed right into the core to stop a chain reaction. To start the reactor, the control rods are partly withdrawn. To increase power, they are withdrawn further. To reduce power, they are pushed back in.

The reactor also has a substance called a moderator, which fills the spaces between the fuel rods in fuel assemblies. The moderator slows down neutrons as they pass from one fuel rod to another, so they cause more fission. A coolant is pumped through the reactor core.

Many reactors use water as the coolant, but some use carbon dioxide gas. The circulating coolant is heated up and carries the heat to an energy conversion system. So the coolant keeps the fuel assemblies from becoming too hot and also transfers the fuel's energy to a steam generator.

An assembly of fuel rods for a pressurized water reactor is checked at a factory in France.

Pressurized water reactors

Sixty per cent of the world's reactors are PWRs (pressurized water reactors). There are also boiling water reactors (21 per cent), pressurized heavy water reactors (ten per cent) and gas cooled reactors (four per cent). In a PWR, the water heated by the core is under great pressure, which allows it to become hotter than normal before it boils.

A PWR has fuel assemblies of 200-300 rods each, arranged vertically in the core, and a large reactor uses 80-100 tonnes of uranium. Heat from the pressurized water boils more water in a steam generator. The high-pressure water is pumped back to the core, where it is heated up again. The steam created drives the blades of a turbine, connected to an electric generator. The steam cools, changes back into water and returns to the steam generator.

Moving nuclear material

Nuclear material has to be transported between fuel plants (for mining, milling, conversion, enrichment and reprocessing), as well as to reactors. Environmental groups are very concerned about this, in case of radioactive contamination. They fear a major disaster. But the World Nuclear Association says: 'About 20 million packages of all sizes containing radioactive materials are routinely transported worldwide annually on public roads, railways and ships. These use robust and secure containers. At sea, they are generally carried in purpose-built ships. Since 1971 there have been more than 20,000 shipments of spent fuel and high-level wastes (over 50,000 tonnes) over more than 30 million kilometres. There has never been any accident in which a container with highly radioactive material has been breached, or has leaked.'

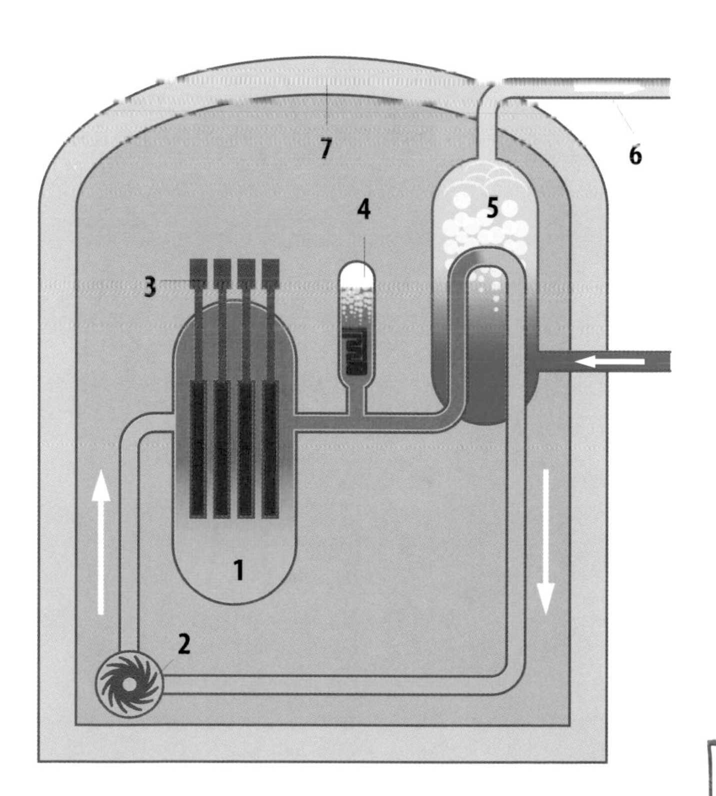

This diagram of a pressurized water reactor shows how the water heated by the reactor is separate from the water in the steam generator system.

PRESSURIZED WATER REACTOR

1 Reactor core
2 Coolant pump
3 Fuel rods
4 Pressurizer
5 Steam generator
6 Steam pumped to turbine, which generates electricity
7 Containment building

The reactor core of a French nuclear power plant.

What happens to used fuel

The fuel assemblies in nuclear power plants need replacing every year or two. Spent fuel still gives off both heat and radiation, so it has to be handled very carefully. The fuel assemblies are usually cooled in storage pools near the reactor. The water in the pools absorbs the heat and shields the radiation. Used fuel may be kept in pools for several months or years. Then it is prepared for permanent disposal or reprocessing.

Reprocessing fuel

This is the chemical operation that separates fuel for recycling from nuclear waste. The metallic outer casing of the spent fuel rods is stripped away and they are dissolved in nitric acid. This produces material that is about 96 per cent uranium (95 per cent U-238 and one per cent U-235), three per cent highly radioactive waste and one per cent plutonium.

The uranium can be converted and enriched, then reused as nuclear fuel. The plutonium can be made into mixed oxide fuel (or MOX) which is used in some reactors. Major commercial reprocessing plants in France, Russia and the UK process 5000 tonnes of used fuel per year. France and the UK also reprocess nuclear waste from other countries.

Nuclear waste

There are no long-term storage facilities for nuclear waste yet. Many experts believe the best solution is to bury waste deep underground, away from earthquake zones and volcanoes. The USA has decided on such a site at Yucca Mountain in Nevada, and in 2007 the US Department of Energy announced that it wanted the site to store 135,000 tonnes of waste. The repository will be 300 metres beneath the mountain. But it will not be ready to accept nuclear waste until 2017, and it is opposed by many people in Nevada. Other countries, such as Sweden and Finland, have also chosen sites, and experts have suggested that Australia and Russia would be suitable locations.

An everlasting problem?

One of the reasons many people are concerned about nuclear waste is that it continues to be hazardous for so long. In the waste there are small amounts (0.3 per cent) of substances such as caesium and strontium. These substances remain dangerously radioactive for about 600 years. But plutonium is even more of a long-term worry. It can remain radioactive for thousands of years. Even small amounts of plutonium can cause genetic damage and cancer in humans. Waste disposal is one of the biggest issues related to nuclear power.

The nuclear industry claims there is no urgency, since the amount of nuclear waste is still relatively small. The World Nuclear Association says there are about 270,000 tonnes of spent fuel in storage, mostly at reactor sites. About 12,000 tonnes are added every year, of which 3000 tonnes go for reprocessing.

This house, near the planned repository at Yucca Mountain in Nevada, was destroyed by nuclear weapons tests in the 1950s.

Nuclear power around the world

In 2008 there were 439 commercial nuclear power reactors operating in 30 countries around the world. Together they supply 16 per cent of the world's electricity, and the nuclear industry aims to increase that to 17 per cent by 2020. But the way nuclear-generated electricity is produced and used varies enormously.

At one end of the scale, France uses nuclear power to produce more than three quarters of its electricity. In three other European countries – Belgium, Lithuania and Slovakia – the figure is more than half. At the other end of the scale, there are no reactors at all in Australia, the whole of Africa (except for two in South Africa), much of south-west and south-east Asia, and European countries such as Italy, Austria, Greece and Poland.

The world's top ten nuclear countries in terms of the percentage of electricity they generate include eight from Europe and two from Asia (Armenia and South Korea).

Country	No of reactors	Electricity in TWh	Percentage of electricity
France	59	428.7	78.1
Lithuania	1	7.9	72.3
Slovakia	5	16.6	57.2
Belgium	7	44.3	54.4
Sweden	10	65.0	48.0
Ukraine	15	84.8	47.5
Bulgaria	2	18.1	43.6
Armenia	1	2.4	42.0
Slovenia	1	5.3	40.3
South Korea	20	141.2	38.6

The top producers

The United States is the leading national producer of nuclear-generated electricity, with 30 per cent of the world total. This is much more than France. Japan comes third, followed by Germany and Russia.

Country	No of reactors	Percentage of country's electricity	Electricity in TWh	Percentage of world nuclear electricity
USA	104	19.4	787.2	29.6
France	59	78.1	428.7	16.1
Japan	55	30.02	291.5	11.0
Germany	17	31.8	158.7	6.0
Russia	31	15.9	144.3	5.4
South Korea	20	38.6	141.2	5.3
Canada	18	15.8	92.4	3.5
Ukraine	15	47.5	84.8	3.2
UK	19	18.4	69.2	2.6
Sweden	10	48.0	65.0	2.4

What is a watt?

A watt (W) is a unit of power, which measures the rate of producing or using energy. The term was named after the Scottish engineer James Watt (1736-1819), who developed an improved steam engine. Watt measured his engine's performance in horsepower (hp). One horsepower equals 746 watts. Today, watts are used to measure electric power.

1 kilowatt (kW) = 1 thousand watts
1 megawatt (MW) = 1 million watts
1 gigawatt (GW) = 1 thousand million watts
1 terawatt (TW) = 1 million million watts.
In the tables TWh stands for terawatt hours and refers to the amount of electricity produced by nuclear energy every hour.

Shutting down safely

Some countries, such as Germany and the UK, are closing down nuclear plants, and this is not easy. Altogether, 90 commercial reactors have shut down worldwide. Some of these have been fully dismantled. The World Nuclear Association says, 'Proven techniques and equipment are available to dismantle nuclear facilities safely and these have now been well demonstrated in several parts of the world. Decommissioning costs for nuclear power plants, including disposal of associated wastes, are reducing.' Others disagree. In the UK, the cost is estimated at £73 billion, and environmental groups fear land contamination.

Workers in North Korea pour concrete for the containment building of a nuclear reactor. There was international support for the North Korean programme, but it has not been completed.

New reactors

Fewer nuclear power plants are being built now than during the 1970s and 1980s. But 34 reactors are under construction in 11 countries, including China, South Korea, Japan and Russia. More than 80 more are scheduled to be built and 200 more have been proposed. Between 1990 and 2006, world nuclear electricity production rose by 40 per cent, partly because reactors became more efficient. The US reactors did best, averaging 90 per cent of maximum output (up from 65 per cent in 1990).

The world nuclear industry

Countries without reactors also form part of the world's nuclear industry. Some are involved at the beginning of the nuclear fuel cycle, which includes uranium mining, milling, conversion, enrichment and fuel fabrication. These countries include top uranium producers Australia,

Kazakhstan and Niger. Others become involved at the later stages, in storage, reprocessing, recycling and disposal. Italy imports more than ten per cent of its electricity from other countries using nuclear power. Italy shut down its reactors as a result of a referendum after the accident at Chernobyl in 1986 (see page 28).

Reacting to oil crises

When a world oil crisis pushed up prices in 1974, the French government decided to expand the country's nuclear power programme. Politicians were influenced by the fact that France had great expertise in engineering but no large energy resources. The nuclear plants allowed the country to import less energy. Through most of the 1970s, France imported more electricity than it exported. Today, it is the world's largest electricity exporter, supplying Italy, the UK and other countries. Electricity is France's fourth largest export, and the country also exports expertise and technology – especially in PWR reactors – to Belgium, China, South Africa and South Korea.

France imports most of its uranium from Canada (36 per cent) and Niger (26 per cent). Its electricity prices are low, which helps to keep nuclear power popular. French experts also claim that their country has an extremely low level of carbon dioxide emissions per head, because more than 90 per cent of its electricity comes from nuclear and hydropower.

Using energy to produce energy

The nuclear fuel cycle uses energy from other sources, such as oil, gas and coal. This energy is used for mining, transporting goods, building power stations, and so on. Anti-nuclear activists are keen to draw attention to this energy use, which counteracts the claim of the nuclear industry that nuclear generation of electricity does not produce greenhouse gases (as burning fossil fuels does). The nuclear industry claims that less than six per cent of nuclear energy output comes from other sources, and that this is 'usually only two to three per cent'. Some researchers have calculated that the CO_2 produced by the complete nuclear fuel cycle is about a third to half of that of a gas fired power station. This is perhaps not as good a comparison as many pro-nuclear activists would like. Comparisons are difficult to make, but it is true to say that the complete cycle is not emission-free.

But French people are concerned about waste disposal. In 2006 new regulations on nuclear materials and waste disposal came into force, which apply until 2021. For high-level waste the French favour deep underground disposal and a new French repository is scheduled to open in 2025.

Nuclear energy in the United States

There are 104 nuclear reactors in the USA. Seven more reactors are planned and a further 25 proposed. All US plants are either pressurized water (PWR) or boiling water (BWR). In 2006 they produced 20 per cent of US electricity, down from 22 per cent ten years earlier.

A government agency called the Nuclear Regulatory Commission, established in 1974, regulates nuclear power production in the US. The agency has to ensure that power plants operate safely and are regularly inspected. It grants licences and has recently extended those of some

The nuclear power plant sites of the United States. They are mostly concentrated in the east of the country. There are no commercial nuclear plants in Alaska or Hawaii.

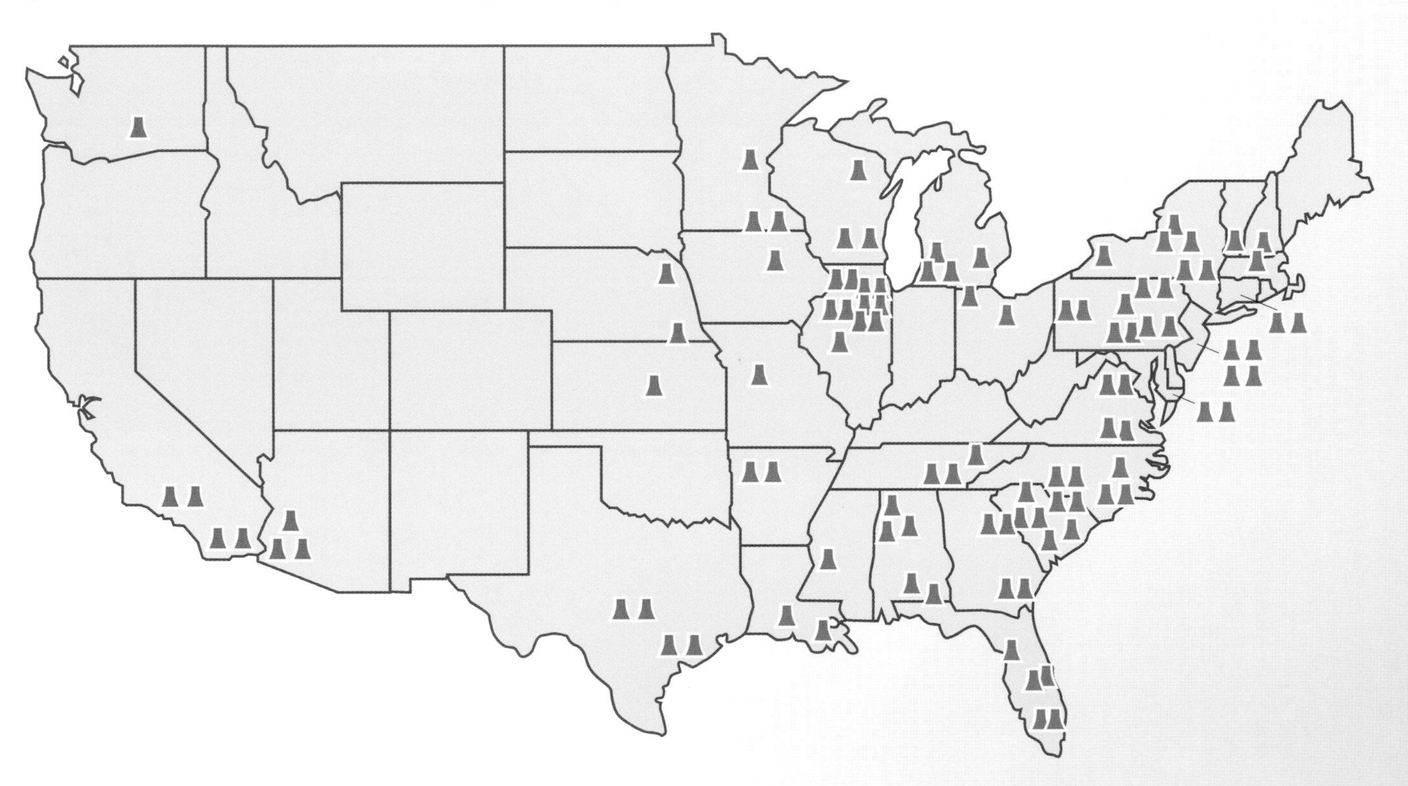

plants for a further 20 years. By 2007 the agency had renewed the licences of 48 reactors. However, as in many other countries, public opinion is divided on whether or not nuclear power should be increased.

A nuclear energy partnership

In 2006, the US Department of Energy announced a new initiative called the Global Nuclear Energy Partnership (GNEP). The GNEP 'seeks to develop worldwide consensus on enabling expanded use of economical, carbon-free nuclear energy to meet growing electricity demand. This will use a nuclear fuel cycle that enhances energy security, while promoting non-proliferation. It would achieve its goal by having nations with secure, advanced nuclear capabilities provide fuel services – fresh fuel and recovery of used fuel – to other nations who agree to employ nuclear energy for power generation purposes only.' By 2008, the GNEP had 21 member countries: Australia, Bulgaria, Canada, China, France, Ghana, Hungary, Italy, Japan, Jordan, Kazakhstan, Lithuania, Poland, Romania, Russia, Senegal, Slovenia, South Korea, Ukraine, the United Kingdom and the United States.

Britain's nuclear energy

In the UK, nuclear power is an important issue. All but one of Britain's 19 existing power stations is likely to be closed by 2023. No reactors have been built since the 1980s and 21 have been decommissioned. But the government has said that rising oil and gas prices and pressure to tackle climate change mean that the country must consider a new generation of reactors. Some believe that nuclear power is needed to secure the UK's future energy supplies, but others believe that more resources should be put into renewable energy.

What do people think?

Opinions on nuclear power are divided. A 2007 survey of people living within 16 km of US nuclear plants found that more than 90 per cent thought nuclear energy was important for the future, 82 per cent favoured it now, 77 per cent said new plants should be built and 71 per cent said they would accept a new plant near their home.

On nuclear waste, 71 per cent thought that storing it at the plant was safe and 78 per cent said that the federal government should carry on developing the Yucca Mountain repository (see page 21). But a different 2007 US poll showed that 65 per cent of people were against nuclear plants, 58 per cent were against fossil fuel plants, and 76 per cent supported developing power from new wind turbines. In the UK, a BBC poll found that 72 per cent were against building new nuclear reactors.

What about safety?

There are safety concerns about all methods of energy production, but safety is a major issue when it comes to nuclear power. There are several reasons for this, and the first is the possibility of an accident at a nuclear reactor. This could have far more catastrophic effects than accidents at other power plants.

Chernobyl, Ukraine, 1986

In the early hours of 26 April 1986, a test was run on one of the four graphite-moderated, water cooled reactors at Chernobyl, north of Kiev in the Ukraine region of what was then the Soviet Union. The controllers running the test did not realize that the reactor had become unstable, and some of the usual safety devices were switched off. When power suddenly surged, a controller pressed a button to insert all the control rods and shut down the reactor, but it was too late. Some fuel rods fractured, the control rods got stuck, and the power quickly became irresistible. Pressure increased and there was a sudden explosion of steam.

The ruins of Chernobyl reactor number 4, photographed in June 1986. The debris was later sealed off.

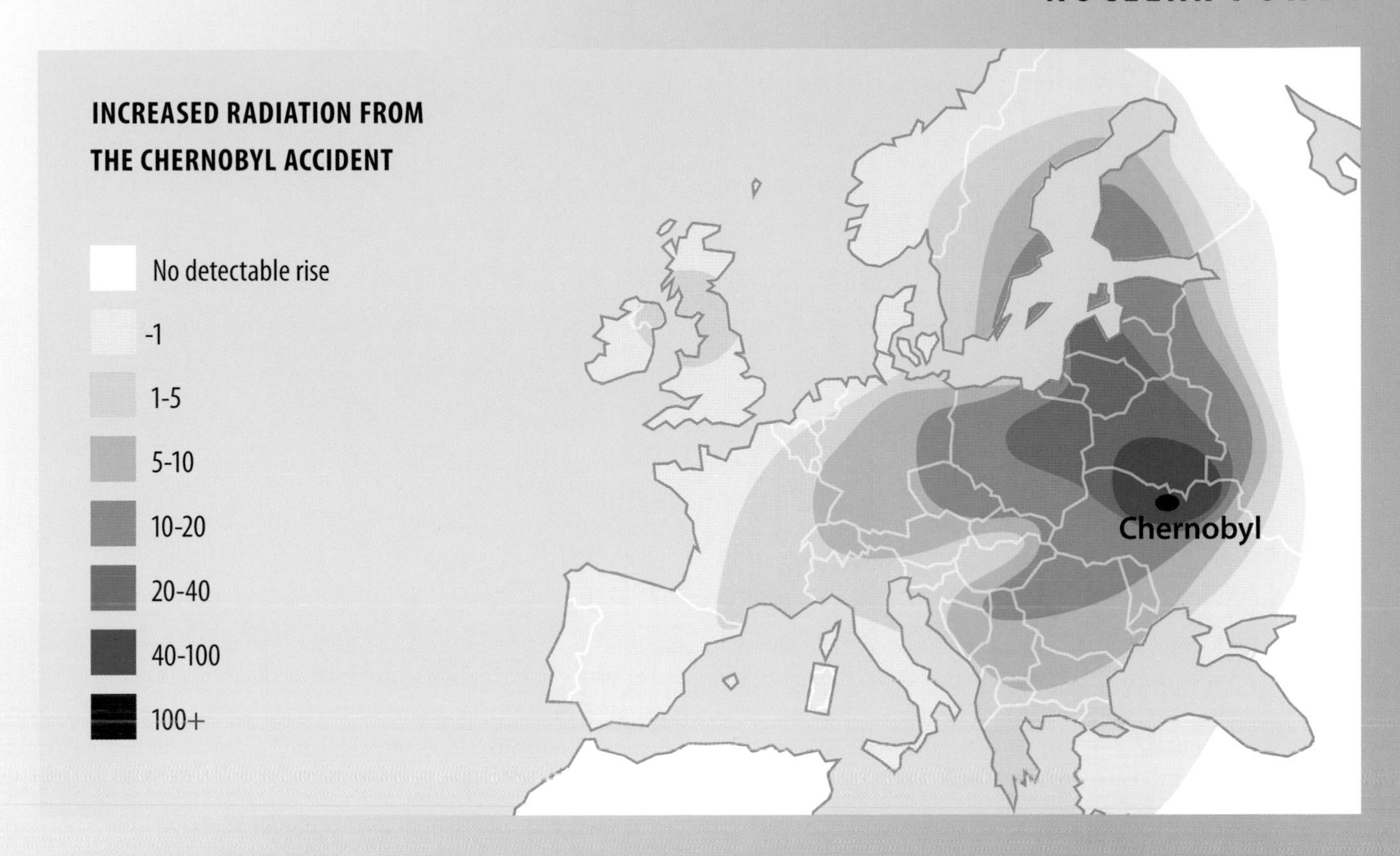

Radiation levels across Europe a week after the accident. The levels are shown in multiples of the normal rate.

This blew off the reactor lid and the roof of the containment building. The explosion caused a fire and threw particles of nuclear fuel and radioactive elements, such as caesium and iodine, into the air in a swirling cloud.

Catastrophic effects

The radioactive plume, or cloud, spread over a wide area. Fallout soon reached parts of Ukraine, Belarus, Moldova and Russia. Radioactivity levels rose as far away as Britain and Ireland. Scientists have estimated that the disaster released a hundred times more radiation than the atom bombs dropped on Nagasaki and Hiroshima in the Second World War.

No one knows exactly how many people died in the accident. A report by the International Atomic Energy Agency and World Health Organization said that 47 members of the emergency services died, because they were not equipped to deal with high levels of radiation. The fire burned for nine days. Nine children have since died of thyroid cancer, and at least 9000 people may die of cancer because of the fallout. The environmental group Greenpeace says its research shows that the death toll will be nearer 100,000.

The future for Chernobyl

The damaged reactor (number 4) was sealed off and covered by a concrete sarcophagus. Construction was stopped on two new reactors (numbers 5 and 6) at the site. Reactor 2 was closed down after a fire in 1991, reactor 1 was decommissioned in 1996, and reactor 3 in 2000. Experts are worried that the concrete sarcophagus could be damaged by a severe storm or an earthquake. In 2007, the decision was made to build an arch-shaped steel casing over the reactor, 200 metres long and 190 metres wide. This will take five years to complete. The damaged reactor can then be completely dismantled.

Radioactivity and health

Facts about the effects of radioactivity are controversial. A report on Chernobyl by the United Nations Scientific Committee on the Effects of Atomic Radiation says, 'There had been up to the year 2002 about 4000 cases of thyroid cancer reported in children and adolescents who were exposed at the time of the accident, and more cases can be expected during the next decades... Apart from this increase, there is no evidence of a major public health impact attributable to radiation exposure 20 years after the accident.' But others believe that radiation effects can be widespread and cause disease decades later.

Research has also been done on the possible effects on health of living near a nuclear power station. The results are confusing. Some surveys have shown a higher risk of leukaemia in children near nuclear facilities, but others have not. The two sides of the nuclear debate use whichever statistics suit their case.

Worst ever nuclear accident

The International Atomic Energy Agency has drawn up a scale for nuclear accidents. The International Nuclear Event Scale (INES) has seven categories:

7 Major accident
6 Serious accident
5 Accident with off-site risk
4 Accident without off-site risk
3 Serious incident
2 Incident
1 Anomaly

Chernobyl was a category 7 event on the INES scale, because it had a large impact beyond the nuclear site, with widespread health and environmental effects. It is considered the worst ever nuclear accident.

More accidents

The world's second most catastrophic nuclear accident – given an INES category 6 – also happened in the Soviet Union. In 1957, there was a problem at the Mayak plant in southern Russia, where nuclear fuel and waste was reprocessed for use in nuclear weapons. The cooling system of a tank of dissolved nuclear waste failed, causing an explosion and releasing radiation. Two hundred people died from radiation sickness, and a further 470,000 people were exposed to radiation. There have been other,

The Windscale advanced gas cooled reactor was opened in 1962 and shut down in 1981. It was nicknamed the 'golf ball' by plant workers.

smaller accidents at Mayak reprocessing plant. In 2007, a faulty tap allowed a leak of radioactive waste, but this was contained within the site.

In 1957 there was a fire at the reprocessing plant at Windscale, in north-west England. Radioactive material – iodine-131 – was released into the environment. However, the British Medical Research Council said that it was unlikely any harm had been done to human health. The accident was rated category 5 on the INES scale. The Windscale plant (later renamed Sellafield as a nuclear complex) is now being decommissioned.

Who to believe?

The nuclear industry claims that it has learned from mistakes made 50 years ago. Modern safety measures are more effective, they say. However, those on the other side of the debate claim that this is a biased interpretation.

In 2007, a Greenpeace International report had this to say about the Russian reprocessing plant: 'Mayak is a horrific example of the true face of the global nuclear industry. The Mayak anniversary [in 2007] must serve as a wake-up call to the world about the real costs of nuclear power, at a time when the nuclear industry is desperately trying to make itself relevant by manipulating the climate crisis, aggressively promoting itself as a low-cost mature technology. Mayak's half-century of contamination history exposes the dirty side of the nuclear spin. If people fall for nuclear spin, then the so-called nuclear renaissance becomes another threat of climate change.'

Accident at Three Mile Island

There was a category 5 accident in 1979 at the Three Mile Island nuclear power plant near Harrisburg, in Pennsylvania, USA. A cooling pump in one of the plant's two reactors failed, and the PWR reactor shut down automatically. This would have been the end of the problem, but unknown to the operators a valve stayed open. This led to the reactor core overheating as fuel rods began to melt. Operators later found that about half the core had melted, but the reactor's containment building did not break or burst. There was concern that radiation might have escaped from the plant. A report later concluded that some radiation had escaped, but that there were no ill-health effects at the time or subsequently. Three Mile Island's damaged reactor 2 has never reopened, but reactor 1 was allowed to start up again in 1985.

The film that predicted disaster

Just 12 days before the Three Mile Island accident, an American film called *The China Syndrome* was released. This was based on a term first used in 1970, suggesting that a nuclear meltdown in the USA might lead to a reactor core burning its way right through the Earth to China (on the opposite side of the globe). Many experts said that this was impossible, but the term China syndrome stuck and still appears in dictionaries.

Three Mile Island power plant lies on an island in the Susquehanna River. The damaged reactor was closed and its core was removed from the site.

Two engineers inspect part of an underground storage facility for nuclear waste. Anti-nuclear protesters have demonstrated against the Gorleben repository in northern Germany.

Waste problems

Nuclear waste is dangerous because it is radioactive. That is why there is such concern about how to dispose of it. But there are other concerns, too. If nuclear material – including nuclear waste – were to fall into the wrong hands, it could be used to make a devastating nuclear device, or dirty bomb. This would be horribly effective for terrorists, who could target nuclear transports for the same reason.

In 2003, the head of the International Atomic Energy Agency warned a security conference that the problem of radioactive material disappearing from official records was especially serious in Russia and the other countries of the former Soviet Union. He said that there had been more than 280 confirmed cases of radioactive material being bought and sold by criminals.

Wasting nuclear waste?

Most people view nuclear waste as a big problem. Some experts, however, think we may be worrying too much and could even be missing an opportunity. In his book *The Revenge of Gaia*, James Lovelock writes: '[The] public belief in the harmfulness of nuclear power is too strong to break by direct argument. Instead, I have offered in public to accept all of the high-level waste produced in a year from a nuclear power station for deposit on my small plot of land; it would occupy a space about a cubic metre in size and fit safely in a concrete pit, and I would use the heat from its decaying radioactive elements to heat my home. It would be a waste not to use it. More important, it would be no danger to me, my family or the wildlife.'

The threat of terrorism

Nuclear plants could become terrorist targets, leading to explosions and the release of radioactive material. This is seen as a danger by governments around the world, which have security plans that are not published. Among the general public, fears about terrorism have increased since the attacks on New York's World Trade Center in September 2001.

Since then, tests have been carried out by the US Electric Power Research Institute that apparently show that nuclear installations can safely survive even an aircraft attack. The tests used a fully-fuelled Boeing 767 aircraft, which made a direct hit on a nuclear containment building. The World Nuclear Association says that no part of the plane or its fuel entered the reactor building, which remained intact.

In another experiment, a rocket-propelled F4 Phantom jet hit a 3.7-metre thick slab of concrete at 765 km/h. The concrete slab was damaged only to a depth of 60 millimetres.

A dramatic photograph of the F4 Phantom test, a split second before the aircraft hit the concrete wall.

Nuclear energy and weapons

The international Treaty on the Non-Proliferation of Nuclear Weapons, which came into force in 1970, allows only five countries to have nuclear weapons: China, France, Russia, the UK and the US. These countries agreed to help other countries benefit from the peaceful use of nuclear energy, but not to produce nuclear weapons. The International Atomic Energy Agency must inspect nuclear facilities in all countries.

Only four countries have not signed the treaty – India, Israel, North Korea and Pakistan – and all are thought to have nuclear weapons. Treaty countries also agree to seek nuclear disarmament, but none of the countries with nuclear arms has given them up yet. This causes another security problem. Countries could claim that they are using nuclear facilities to generate power, but be manufacturing nuclear weapons. In recent years people have had this concern about Iran.

Mohamed ElBaradei chairs an IAEA conference at its headquarters in Vienna, Austria.

Does the International Atomic Energy Agency help?

Newspapers sometimes call the IAEA the United Nations' nuclear watchdog, and most people would agree that the IAEA helps to overcome many world safety concerns. The agency promotes the peaceful use of nuclear energy and tries to reduce its use for military purposes. 'The IAEA is the world's centre of co-operation in the nuclear field. It was set up as the world's Atoms for Peace organization in 1957 within the United Nations family. The agency works with its Member States and multiple partners worldwide to promote safe, secure and peaceful nuclear technologies. The IAEA works for the safe, secure and peaceful uses of nuclear science and technology. Its key roles contribute to international peace and security, and to the World's Millennium Goals for social, economic and environmental development. Three main... areas of work underpin the mission: safeguards and verification [acting as the world's nuclear inspectors]; safety and security [especially protecting people and the environment from harmful radiation exposure]; and science and technology [helping countries develop peaceful applications of nuclear science].' The agency and its director general, Mohamed ElBaradei, were jointly awarded the Nobel Peace Prize in 2005.

Nuclear travel and medicine

During the 1950s, many scientists believed that nuclear power would become the most important energy source of all. They realized that it could preserve food by irradiation and cook it with microwaves. Perhaps most importantly, it could help to cure disease through nuclear medicine.

The decade became known as the Atomic Age, when people also thought that nuclear power held the key for future transport. In 1958 the Ford Motor Company unveiled its Ford Nucleon concept car, powered by a small nuclear reactor instead of a petrol engine. The car never went into production, but by then nuclear ships had taken to the seas.

Opposite: the Russian nuclear icebreaker Yamal *ploughs through Arctic ice on its way to the North Pole.*

The Kursk disaster

Why were nuclear cars never built? And why aren't there more nuclear civilian ships? Cost may be one issue, but probably more important is the public attitude towards nuclear safety. In 2000, the Russian nuclear submarine *Kursk* sank in the Barents Sea after a torpedo explosion on board. Despite rescue attempts, all 118 sailors died. The submarine was raised from the seabed a year later by a special recovery vessel. At a Russian shipyard the reactors were found intact and were defuelled. The fuel was taken to the reprocessing plant at Mayak (see page 30), and the wreck went to a naval storage site. Though there was no apparent contamination, the accident made people more nervous about nuclear propulsion. The *Arktika* icebreaker also had an accident in 2007, when a fire broke out on board. The nuclear reactor was not damaged.

Nuclear submarines

Nuclear reactors need no air and use very little fuel (enriched uranium-235). In a submarine, the reactor produces steam to drive a turbine and turn a propeller shaft. A nuclear sub can stay underwater for a long time without refuelling. The first, *USS Nautilus*, was launched in 1954, and its early voyages broke all records for time and distance travelled underwater. Four years later, the 97.5-metre long submarine reached the North Pole beneath the frozen surface of the Arctic Ocean.

In 1960 the 136-metre long *USS Triton* sailed from New London naval base in Connecticut. This twin-reactor submarine then submerged for 84 days, travelling around the world beneath the surface of the Atlantic, Pacific and Indian oceans. Today, the US, Britain, China, France and Russia all have nuclear-powered submarines in their navies. The Indian navy is building a new type called an ATV (advanced technology vessel).

Surface ships

The first nuclear-powered surface vessel was the Russian icebreaker *Lenin*. Launched in 1957, this ship had three reactors driving separate propellers. Nuclear power is perfect for icebreakers, providing strength for long voyages. In 1977 the *Arktika* became the first surface ship to reach the North Pole. The world's navies have also used nuclear reactors to power cruisers and aircraft carriers. The 342-metre long *USS Enterprise*, launched in 1960, is the longest naval vessel in the world. This huge ship has eight reactors driving four propellers and is still in active service.

Space travel

Deep-space probes and spacecraft exploring the furthest planets in our solar system cannot use solar power for their electrical instruments. Because of this, many spacecraft use radioisotope thermoelectric generators (RTGs). These harness heat produced by the natural decay of radioactive materials. Apollo astronauts used RTGs to power scientific instruments on the Moon.

Now scientists are working on using small nuclear reactors as the primary power source for long-distance spacecraft. Increased speeds could cut a journey to Mars by two thirds. One of NASA's programmes, called Project Prometheus, is investigating nuclear power. One of the options is to use a nuclear thermal rocket, in which hydrogen is heated in a nuclear reactor so that it expands through a rocket nozzle and creates thrust.

An artist's impression of a nuclear-powered unmanned spacecraft approaching Jupiter.

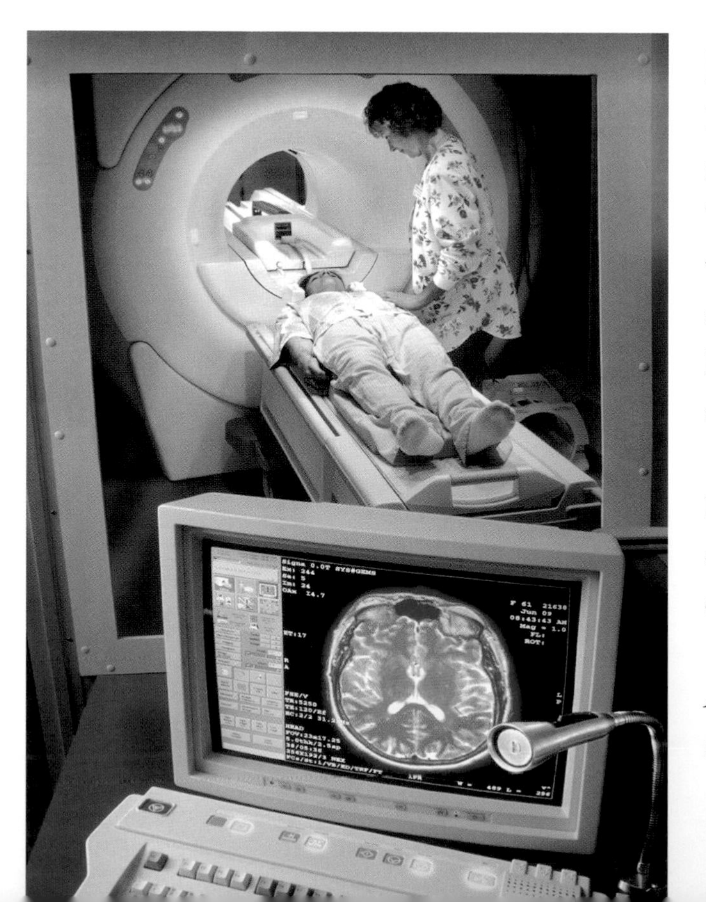

Nuclear medicine

Nuclear medicine uses radioactive isotopes (or radioisotopes) to study, diagnose and treat disease. The radioisotopes are produced in research reactors, which are simpler than power reactors and operate at lower temperatures. Research reactors need highly-enriched uranium but use far less fuel and produce fewer fission products.

Radiotherapy is used to treat many medical conditions, especially cancer, using radiation to destroy targeted cells. Russia has more research

A patient is prepared for a scan that uses safe nuclear technology.

reactors than any other nation, followed by the US, Japan, France and Germany. Since the early 1970s, when many research reactors were built, security concerns have grown, especially as many are at universities and other insecure civilian locations.

Weapons of mass destruction

Few countries in the world have nuclear weapons. According to the Carnegie Endowment for International Peace, in 2007 the estimated numbers of nuclear warheads were as follows.

Russia	**USA**	**China**	**France**	
16,000	10,300	410	350	
UK	**Israel**	**India**	**Pakistan**	**Total**
200	100-170	75-110	50-110	**27,600**

Several countries have given up nuclear weapons. During the 1980s Argentina and Brazil abandoned their weapons programmes. In 1993, South Africa announced that it had dismantled its weapons. In the same year, Belarus, Kazakhstan and Ukraine allowed Russia to remove its nuclear weapons located there. In 2005, North Korea agreed to scrap its weapons programme in exchange for aid. Then in 2006 North Korea said it had successfully tested a nuclear weapon, though it has since reported that it has shut down its main reactor.

Nuclear power versus disarmament

Many people who believe in total nuclear disarmament also believe that nuclear power should not be used for other purposes either. They say that if nuclear material exists, warmongers will always find a way to make bombs with it. The Campaign for Nuclear Disarmament (CND) says: 'The proliferation of nuclear weapons is inextricably linked to nuclear power by a shared need for enriched uranium, and through the generation of plutonium as a by-product of spent nuclear fuel. The two industries have been linked since the very beginning and a nuclear weapons free world requires a non-nuclear energy policy.'

Do you agree? And if we stopped using nuclear power altogether, how could we be sure that nuclear weapons did not still exist secretly somewhere?

What does the future hold?

Nuclear power is controversial, and its future hangs in the balance. This might change, depending on developing technologies and new approaches to problems such as nuclear waste. There may also be changes in attitude towards using fossil fuels and more modern methods of renewable energy.

New generation reactors

A new generation of fission reactors is being built. Manufacturers and pro-nuclear groups claim that the advanced (or generation-3) designs have many advantages over previous models. They have a modular construction, which means that components are built elsewhere and shipped to the reactor site. Engineers say that they have simplified designs and cut construction and generation costs.

Safety measures have improved. In the event of a problem, passive safety systems use natural forces such as gravity, circulation and evaporation, rather than active systems such as pumps, motors and valves. Experts claim that these more efficient reactors will generate just ten per cent of the waste produced by earlier reactors.

Futuristic fusion

Nuclear fusion devices are still experimental. Engineers have built test reactors, but so far they have not proved practical. Between 1985 and 1999, scientists in California used a laser-driven reactor to produce fusion. An incredible amount of power in the form of heat and light could be concentrated on nuclear fuel for just a billionth of a second, causing nuclei to fuse (and give off energy). Other test reactors are called tokamaks, from the Russian for 'a doughnut-shaped chamber'. In 2006 China, the European Union, India, Japan, Russia, South Korea and the US agreed to work together to fund a nuclear fusion project based in France, called ITER (International Thermonuclear Experimental Reactor). The project aims to produce an experimental tokamak reactor that will lead to a full-scale commercial power plant by 2050.

Opposite: this tokamak fusion reactor is being tested at a research establishment in Japan.

Is nuclear power the right priority?

Pro-nuclear groups say yes, because without it there will be an energy gap. They believe that renewable sources will not produce enough power to meet our energy needs.

However, Greenpeace answers the question in the following way: 'The 439 operating commercial nuclear reactors currently supply around 15 [or 16] per cent of global electricity. This represents only 6.5 per cent of [the] world's overall energy consumption. Even maintaining this current share would require a massive new build programme... Doubling the existing installed nuclear capacity of 372,000 megawatts by 2030 would mean building hundreds of new reactors. Yet this would hardly increase the nuclear energy share in the world's total energy consumption beyond ten per cent and would reduce total greenhouse emissions by less than five per cent. Achieving even this small slice of world energy supply would require an unrealistically ambitious plan: a large new nuclear reactor would need to be built and come on line every two weeks from now [2007] until 2030.'

We all have to make up our own minds on the subject.

Gearing up or down?

Different countries have varying views on the future of nuclear power. Countries such as France want to continue to increase nuclear electricity, but its neighbour Germany has decided to shut down all its reactors by 2020. The German government is investing more in renewable sources, such as wind and solar power, but opponents say the country will face an energy gap if new nuclear plants are not built. China and Russia want to build more nuclear power stations, while Britain is uncertain.

Future costs

It is difficult to predict how costs will change in future. Pro-nuclear groups say that costs will continue to go down, but anti-nuclear groups claim this is because of government subsidies (which they think are unfair to renewable energy sources). Today the cost of nuclear-generated electricity is similar to that of fossil fuels, and oil and gas prices are likely to go on rising in the near future. Opponents to nuclear power point out the high cost of building, securing and decommissioning reactors, and of protecting and disposing of waste. Forecasts suggest that each new advanced power plant would cost between £400 million and £1 billion.

The challenge of global warming

We know we are adding to a natural greenhouse effect by emitting so many waste gases from power plants, factories and cars. Many of these greenhouse gases – especially carbon dioxide – are produced when we burn coal, oil or gas to release energy. Much of our energy use adds to global warming, so land, sea and air temperatures are gradually increasing. This is a great concern because global warming is causing ice sheets to melt and sea levels to rise, as well as more heatwaves, droughts and severe weather such as hurricanes. However, nuclear reactors do not emit greenhouse gases (although the whole nuclear fuel cycle does, see page 25). This makes the nuclear option attractive to many people. Opponents maintain that this takes resources away from the most important energy option – renewable sources.

The glaciers of Los Glaciares National Park in Argentina are slowly melting as global temperatures rise.

Planning ahead for nuclear development

One of the big problems for politicians is that it takes a long time to build a nuclear power station. Decisions have to be made many years in advance, and by the time the power station is ready people's attitudes may have changed, the overall energy situation might be different, and a new government might be in power. Experts claim that new advanced reactors can be built in three to four years, but sites have to be agreed, licences granted, security issues explored, and tests run on the new power plant. That is why many politicians talk about a lead time of at least ten years.

Glossary

atom The basic particle of all matter.
centrifuge A device that spins rapidly and separates different substances.
consensus General agreement.
control rod A rod that absorbs neutrons and can be inserted into a nuclear reactor to slow down fission.
decommission To take something out of service.
diffusion Spreading out.
dirty bomb A bomb that uses explosives to spread radioactive nuclear material over a wide area.
electron A particle that occurs in atoms, circling the nucleus; it has a negative electric charge.
element A substance that cannot be separated into a simpler form.
emission Producing and giving off something (such as a waste gas); also the waste gas produced and given off.
enrichment Making something (such as an isotope) more powerful.
fallout Radioactive dust created by a nuclear explosion.
fission Splitting an atomic nucleus.
fusion Joining together of atomic nuclei.
generator A machine that turns mechanical energy into electrical energy.
hydropower Electricity generated using water power.
irradiation Treating food with radiation to make it last longer.
isotope The form of an element with a particular number of neutrons (such as uranium-235, which has 143 neutrons).
leukaemia A type of cancer of the blood.
licence Official permission to do something.
mass The amount of matter in something.
moderator A substance that slows neutrons in a nuclear reactor.
neutron A particle that occurs in nuclei; it has no electric charge.
non-proliferation Preventing the increase or spread (of nuclear weapons).
non-renewable energy Energy that is used up and cannot be replaced (from sources such as uranium, oil, coal or gas).
plutonium A radioactive metallic element (symbol Pu).

proton A particle that occurs in nuclei; it has a positive electric charge.
radiation The giving off of high-energy particles by radioactive substances; or energy transmitted in this way.
radioactive Describing a substance such as uranium that has unstable atoms that give off energy in the form of streams of particles.
radium A radioactive metallic element (symbol Ra).
radon A radioactive gaseous element (symbol Rn).
reactor A device in which nuclear reactions are produced to release energy.
referendum A people's vote on a question put by the government.
regulate To organize and control something.
renewable energy Sources of energy that do not run out when used, such as biomass, geothermal, solar, water and wind power.
repository A place where something is stored.
sarcophagus A thick concrete cover that completely encloses something.
thermonuclear Relating to nuclear reactions that occur at very high temperatures.
thyroid cancer A serious disease affecting the thyroid gland in the neck.
watchdog A group that watches over something to see that it is done properly.
yellowcake A concentrated form of uranium oxide.

Websites

BBC guide to the nuclear fuel cycle (with animation of fission) and new reactors
http://news.bbc.co.uk/1/shared/spl/hi/sci_nat/05/nuclear_fuel/html/mining.stm
http://news.bbc.co.uk/1/hi/sci/tech/5165182.stm

The International Atomic Energy Agency official site
www.iaea.org

The World Nuclear Association's view of the nuclear debate and safety
www.world-nuclear.org/info/inf50.html
www.world-nuclear.org/info/inf06.html

Greenpeace's views on nuclear power
www.greenpeace.org/international/campaigns/nuclear

Index